Table of Contents

Sources, Color Mixes, General Instructions, and Color Conversion Chart Pages 4-7

Peaches, Flowers, and Berries on Tile - Clock and Serving Tray

Pages 8-13

Peaches Floral on Small Bowl

Pages 14-15

Strawberries and Blueberries Metal Bowl

Pages 16-17

Strawberries and Blueberries on Glass Bowl with Lid

Pages 18-19

Country Canisters and Lotion Dispenser

Pages 20-23

Winter's Glory

Pages 25-26

Angel T-Light

Page 27

Porcelain Ornament: O Christmas Tree

Pages 28-29

Porcelain Ornament: Dressing Up Frosty

Pages 30-31

Porcelain Ornament: Wishing Upon A Star

Pages 32-33

Porcelain Ornaments: Patriotic

Pages 34-35

Miss Liberty

Pages 36-39

Serenity

Pages 40-43

Sources

Viking Woodcrafts, Inc.
1317 8th Street SE
Waseca, MN 56093
Ph: (800) 328-0116
Fax: (507) 835-3895
E-mail: viking@vikingwoodcrafts.com
Web: www.vikingwoodcrafts.com
Clock frame and serving tray, glass bowl with lid, metalware, wooden stars, lotion dispenser

Gold Seal Products
Cindy Webb
3215 Parkhill Drive
Colorado Springs, CO 80910
Ph: (719) 633-2188
Web: www.goldsealproducts.com
Porcelain stars, round disks, miniature ornaments

Rynne China Company
222 West Eight Mile Road
Hazel Park, MI 48030
Ph: (248) 542-9400
Fax: (248) 542-0047
E-mail: info@rynnechina.com
Web: www.rynnechina.com
Canisters

Brenda Stewart
228 Yorkshire Drive
Williamsburg, VA 23185
Ph: (757) 564-7093
E-mail: BStewartBD@aol.com
Web: www.brendastewart.com
Porcelain plate

Silver Brush Limited
P.O. Box 414
Windsor, NJ 08561-0414
Ph: (609) 443-4900
Fax: (609) 443-4888
E-mail: info@silverbrush.com
Web: www.silverbrush.com

Meisel Hardware Specialties
P.O. Box 70
Mound, MN 55364-0070
Ph: (800) 441-9870
Web: www.meiselwoodhobby.com
Quartz movement and hands

Diamond Drill and Tool Division
AmeriGlas Stained Glass
P.O. Box 27668
Omaha, NE 68127-0668
E-mail: sales@diamonddrillandtool.com
Web: www.diamonddrillandtool.com
Diamond Drill Bit

Lowe's Home Improvement Center
12" sq. unglazed tile

Quilt Cottage
147 Front Street
Swansboro, NC 28584
Ph: (910) 325-1125
E-mail: quilts@clis.com
Retail: Angel T-Light Holder

Sunny Gifts (USA), Inc.
2315 S. Santa Fe
Los Angeles, CA 90058
Ph: (323) 583-8508
Fax: (323) 583-8782
E-mail: info@sunnygiftsusa.com
Web: www.sunnygiftsusa.com
Wholesale: Angel T-Light Holder

Project Designs and Text: Copyright ©2007 Sharon Shannon • Book Design, Illustration & Layout: Copyright ©2007 Viking Woodcrafts, Inc. All rights reserved under Pan American and International copyright conventions. Questions? Visit http://en.wikipedia.org/wiki/Copyright
ISBN-10 0-9786331-8-0; ISBN-13 978-0-9786331-8-9

Disclaimer: The information in this book is presented in good faith. Since the author and publisher have no control over the application of the information presented, we cannot guarantee results. Due to the limitations of the printing process, the colors of the original pieces may differ from the photos contained within, and the finished projects may look slightly different than those pictured. The author and publisher are not responsible for any claims against the user for copyright or patent infringement.

Canister Color Mixes:

Hunter Green
Light Blue
Ultra White
(1:1:1)

Hunter Green
Light Blue
Ultra White
Royal Purple
(1:1:1:1)

Light Blue
Ultra White
(1:1)

Hunter Green
Ultra White
Royal Purple
(2:2:1)

Hunter Green
Royal Purple
(3:1)

Hunter Green
Royal Purple
Ultra White
(1:t:t)

Hunter Green
Ultra White
(3:1)

Hunter Green
Ultra White
(1:1)

Hunter Green
Olive
(1:1)

Hunter Green
Olive
Ultra White
(1:1:t)

Olive
Ultra White
(1:t)

Harvest Orange
Ultra White
(1:1)

Winter's Glory Color Mixes:

Red Iron Oxide
Chocolate
(2:1)

Red Iron Oxide
Chocolate
Ultra White
(2:1:1)

Chocolate
Marshmallow
(2:1)

Hunter Green
Classic Navy Blue
(3:1)

Strawberry Bowl Color Mixes:

Hunter Green
Ultra White
(3:1)

Hunter Green
Ultra White
(3:2)

Hunter Green
Olive
Ultra White
(1:1:t)

Hunter Green
Olive
Ultra White
Chocolate
(1:1:t:t)

Ultra White
Classic Navy Blue
(1:t)

Ultra White
Dark Goldenrod
(3:1)

Hunter Green
Royal Purple
(2:1)

Harvest Orange
Royal Purple
(1:1)

Ultra White
Harvest Orange
(1:1)

Dark Goldenrod
Harvest Orange
(1:1)

General Instructions

Mediums
I use a painting medium along with the paint for all applications. Load your brush with the medium and then wipe lightly on a paper towel before picking up the paint on your brush. Blend on your palette paper. Sometimes I use different mixes of mediums. Whatever the medium used, it is most important to let each application of paint dry before applying another, unless otherwise indicated.

When a large amount of a paint mix is needed, I put the mix into a clean, empty paint bottle to keep it from drying out. (Serenity and the Strawberries and Blueberries Metal Bowl are two projects where storing initial basebcoat mixes would come in handy.) If it is a small amount, I use a bubble from the bubble palette, and I add one drop of Retarder to the paint for the same reason. Also, I put on my palette paper only a small amount of paint at a time, for it will dry up quickly.

For lettering and fine lines, weaken the paint with Thinner. You can also use the Retarder.

When painting is completed, apply a couple of coats of Satin Glaze plus a couple of drops of Thinner added to the surface.

PermEnamel Retarder
Use to extend drying time for additional shading and blending. I use the Retarder as my painting medium most of the time. I add a couple of drops to the palette's bubble of paint to keep it from drying out quickly, and I also dress my brush with it and gently blot on a paper towel before picking up paint. Blend your color paint and Retarder well on the palette paper, just as if you were using regular paint with water. This will allow for smooth floats, and the color seemingly melts into the surface, instead of standing on top.

Have one bubble full of just Retarder, and always remember to have at least one drop of Retarder mixed into each bubble of paint to keep it from drying out too quickly. Dip the brush into the Retarder and blot lightly on a paper towel. Pick up the paint, and blend on the palette paper. This will allow the paint to flow better on the surface, and it will look soft, not harsh. I have Retarder in my brush at all times. When I apply tints, I add a little more Retarder along with the paint on my brush and work the brush on the palette several times. Apply with light touches. It is always better to go light and add more if needed. When you are stippling, for example, bushes: You will know you have too much Retarder if you see bubbles in the paint when stippling on the palette paper. In which case just tap the brush on a paper towel to remove excess.

PermEnamel Satin Glaze or Clear Glass Glaze
Use as a protective topcoat after your painting is completed. I add a drop or two of the Thinner to the glaze and mix it well for an easier application. This is also good to use as a medium for blending and shading on unglazed ceramic tile.

Do not mix the glaze into the paint, but rather keep a small amount in the bubble palette. Add a drop of Retarder into the paint to keep it from drying out too quickly in the bubble palette. Dip a brush into the glaze and pat-blend lightly on both sides just to get rid of the excess. Sideload the brush with paint, and blend on palette paper. Apply color and then extend color out by pitty-patting. I also keep a little of the basecoat color that the area was based in, in one of the bubbles in my palette, in case I need to pat-blend that color back to create a soft transition of color. On some areas of the design, the area is based by pat-blending the colors together where indicated. On other areas I based lightly, before pat-blending the highlights and shades. In either case, I have a bit of glazing medium mix on my brush with the paint. This also keeps the basecoating from looking heavy. For a very light shade, I work my brush on my palette several times for a soft look. I like to use less paint and build up the colors.

PermEnamel Surface Conditioner
Whatever surface you are painting, whether it be glass, tile, china, or metal, it is very important to apply the Surface Conditioner first to prime your surface. Clean the surface with soapy water. Rinse and dry thoroughly. Brush on Conditioner and let dry. Do not rinse or wipe off. When you are painting on glass, this product has a life of four hours, so you will want to apply this on only the area that you will be able to have basecoated in that time frame. Once the area is basecoated, you do not need to reapply the Conditioner.

PermEnamel Thinner
Use PermEnamel Thinner to thin your paint and glazes for easier detailing and line work. This also works well to clean your brushes between applying different colors. You do need to clean the brushes often. I also keep a small amount of this in my bubble palette. Just clean the brush and wipe on a paper towel. You can use water to clean the brush, but be sure to dry well on a paper towel before using.

Surfaces
Ceramic Tiles
Home improvement stores have a beautiful collection of tiles. Because not all tiles are the same exact size, even if they *say* they are 12" square, they may be off a little. It is best if you take the wood piece with you (See Peaches, Flowers and Berries on Tile — Clock and Serving Tray) to the store and fit the tile into it, before purchasing. The tile I used has a stone faux-finish look and was unglazed. Your tile may not be exactly like mine, but you should be able to find one close to it.

Ceramic Tiles, Preparation
Wash the tile with soapy water. Rinse and dry well. Apply the Surface Conditioner and let dry. The technique used for painting on ceramic tile that does not have a high-gloss finish is primarily pat-blending. These tiles are wonderful to paint on. There are many varieties to choose from, and they have beautiful backgrounds. I use the Satin Glaze plus a drop of Retarder mixed into it as my floating and blending medium.

Ceramic Tiles, Drilling with a Diamond Drill Bit
When drilling a hole in the ceramic tile (Peaches, Flowers, and Berries

Clock, for the attachment of the hands) use diamond bits, as hollow bits have a tendency to walk. The bits should be water-cooled to keep them from dulling. Here is what I do. It may sound complex, but it takes only five minutes:
1. Use a drill press to keep the bit from walking.
2. Draw a 1/4" circle in the center of the tile.
3. Lay out a shallow cake pan that will allow the tile to lie flat in the pan; 1" deep is ok.
4. Put a smooth, flat 1/4"-thick piece of wood into the cake pan, and lay the tile on top of the wood.
5. Center the tile under the drill bit, and clamp down.
6. Drill slowly, pouring a little water every few seconds on the tile hole. This will take about 30 seconds.

China
First prepare the china canisters with Surface Conditioner. Next, apply a coat of Satin Glaze (plus a couple drops of Thinner added) over the area that you are going to paint. Let this dry well. The glaze will allow the surface to have more tooth, and the pattern will trace on better. Be careful not to overlap layers of the glaze. It will pull if it has not dried. If you are not sure where you started, it is best to do small sections at a time, letting it dry thoroughly before continuing. The medium I use with the paint is the Retarder.

Metalware
The metal items I used in this book were already primed, so all I did was apply the Surface Conditioner and was ready to paint. If you need to have a piece of metal primed, Delta also has Air-Dry PermEnamel Metal Primer.

Porcelain
Although porcelain pieces have no need for preparation, wash them with soapy water, rinse them well, and let them dry. Many times they have a residue of oil from handling them which the eye cannot see. Apply the Surface Conditioner to the piece and let dry. Note: When you are painting on porcelain, the color will appear lighter as compared to another type of surface.

Wood
Before staining, sand the wood and remove all sanding dust with a tack cloth. You may use the products of your choice, but this is the stain I used: McClosky Stain Controller, following manufacturer's instructions. Do not let it dry before applying the stain. To stain: Mix Burnt Umber oil paint thinned down a little with Turpinoid. Apply with a sponge brush, and let it sit for a few minutes. Wipe off (following the wood's grain) with a clean, soft cloth. (I use my husband's old T-shirts.) Sometimes I have to apply the stain twice to get the effect I want. Since this is an oil-based stain, I let it dry overnight before applying the pattern. You can also lightly spray it with Krylon 1311 Matte Finish Spray before applying the pattern.

Techniques
Basecoating/basecoat
Applying one or two thin coats of paint, often the initial layers of color in an area. Throughout the instructions, you may see the shortened term "base" used for basecoat or basecoating.

Base-tinting
Base-tinting is similar to basecoating, except that you float the color around the design, leaving some of the background showing. This gives you a natural highlight even with a wash of color over it.

Floating
I use soft floats of color for shading and highlighting unless otherwise indicated. Load the corner of the brush with paint and medium and stroke the brush on the palette (no more than 1 or 2 inches) to blend the color. Turn the brush over and stroke it some more. I do this several times to soften the color. You should have a gradual fading across the bristles of the brush.

Pat-blending
When two colors are merging, there should be no defined break between the two colors. Lightly patting these two colors together will alleviate the defined line. Pick up the basecoat color and pat-blend that color back into the shade for a soft transition of color.

Pitty-patting
Applying short little applications of color with a flat or angle brush.

Stippling
To pounce up and down with the tip of the brush on the surface.

Tinting
Applying just a hint of color with a soft float.

Touch (t)
Throughout the instructions you will see "(t)," which means to use just a touch of that color in mixes.

Transfer Paper, Use of
I found that Saral Transfer Paper works very well for all of the projects. When using the grey, be sure you transfer lightly. If the lines appear too dark, go over them with a kneaded eraser. The red, white, and blue colors are also used among the projects in this book.

Color Conversion Chart

PermEnamel	Delta Ceramcoat
Marshmallow	Lt. Ivory
Ultra White	White
Raw Sienna	Raw Sienna
Hunter Green	Dk. Foliage Green
Harvest Orange	Adobe Red + Poppy Orange + Tuscan Red (1:1:1)
Light Burgundy	Burgundy Rose
Red Iron Oxide	Red Iron Oxide
Chocolate	Dk. Chocolate
Ultra Black	Black
Classic Navy Blue	Blue Velvet + Purple Smoke + Purple (1:2:2)
Latte	Latte
Olive	Avocado + Med. Foliage Green (1:1)
Burnt Sienna	Burnt Sienna + Spice Brown (1:1)
Eggplant	Eggplant + Black (6:1)
Maize	Butter Yellow
Candlelight	Candlelight
Mushroom	Lichen Grey
Country Tomato	Tomato Spice + Burnt Sienna (1:1)
Light Peach	Fleshtone #2019 + Dunes Beige (3:1)
14K Gold (Metallic)	Metallic 14K Gold
Victorian Rose	Gypsy Rose
Red Red	Opaque Red
Midnight	Blue Storm + Cadet Blue (4:1)
Silver Smoke	Rain Grey + White + Dolphin Grey (3:1:1)
Dark Goldenrod	Pigskin
Light Blue	Blue Heaven
Royal Purple	Purple
Tropical Purple	Bahama Purple
Ivory	Ivory

Peaches, Flowers, and Berries
On Tile — Clock and Serving Tray

Palette

Delta Air-Dry PermEnamel
(for ceramic pieces)
Burnt Sienna
Candlelight
Chocolate
Country Tomato
Eggplant
Harvest Orange
Hunter Green
Latte
Light Peach
Maize
Mushroom
Olive
Raw Sienna
Ultra White
Air-Dry PermEnamel Retarder
Air-Dry PermEnamel Satin Glaze
Air-Dry PermEnamel Surface Conditioner
Air-Dry PermEnamel Thinner

Delta Ceramcoat
(for wooden tray and clock frame)
Barn Red
Black Green
Burnt Sienna
Burnt Umber
Candy Bar Brown
Dark Chocolate
Dark Foliage Green
Ivory
Light Ivory
Metallic Kim Gold
Napthol Crimson
Persimmon
Raw Sienna
Straw
Wedgwood Green
Gel Blending Medium

Brushes

Silver Brush Limited
Golden Natural Series 2000S #2 Round
Golden Natural Series 2003S #4, #6, #8 Filbert
Golden Natural Series 2006S 1/8", 1/4", 1/2" Angular
Golden Natural Series 2008S 3/4" Square Wash
Ultra Mini Series 2407S #20/0 Script
Crystal Series 6807S #10/0 Script Liner

Supplies

Clock Frame Item #20-10827 and Serving Tray Item #20-10814, available from Viking Woodcrafts, Inc.

2 ceramic tiles, 12" square, unglazed, that look as if they have a faux-finish background, available at Lowe's Home Improvement Center

7/16" Quartz Movement #5168, 3 3/8" Black Serp. Hands #5407, available from Meisel Hardware Specialties

Stain of your choice or McCloskey Stain Controller, Turpenoid, and Burnt Umber oil paint

Diamond Drill and Tool 5/16" (8.1mm)
Diamond Core Drill Bit #DT-508

Krylon 1311 Matte Finish Spray
Blair Satin Tole Spray
Fine sand paper
Tack cloth
Soft, lint-free cloth
Bubble palette used with palette paper
Grey and white transfer paper

See front cover for full picture of clock.

Instructions
Please read the General Instructions.
Medium used with the paint: Satin Glaze plus a drop of Retarder in a bubble of the palette.

Wash and dry the tiles. Brush on the Surface Conditioner with a clean, dry brush. Let dry.

Serving Tray Tile
Before applying the pattern with grey transfer paper, measure the border of the tile with a pencil lightly. Come in from the edge 1/2", and from that line, measure in 1". Transfer the pattern with grey transfer paper. Erase any pencil lines that come into the main fruit areas.

Peaches
The colors for the peaches are:
Mix #1, Medium: Light Peach + Harvest Orange (3:1)
Mix #2, Dark: Mix #1 with a touch of Country Tomato
Light: Maize

With the #8 filbert, basecoat the peaches as illustrated in step one on the worksheet. Blend where the colors meet. Remember to have a bit of glazing medium mix on the brush to keep the paint flowing better and to keep the painting soft. As you are pat-blending these colors together, wipe the brush on a paper towel before picking up the next color. See worksheet.

Using the 1/4" angular brush, wash Country Tomato in the dark areas, not extending out as far as the first placement of Mix #2. In the darkest blush area of the peach, pat-blend some Eggplant + a touch of Ultra White added. Extend this color out here and there a bit. This not only softens the appearance, but also gives the peach skin that bruised look. Let dry. Then add a tad of Eggplant + Country Tomato (1:1), in the center of the blush and in the V areas of the darkest shade placement. Using the #6 filbert, pat-blend the highlight on the peach with Mix #1 with a touch of Ultra White added. Renforce the Maize areas if needed, and wash a bit on the right side of the peach that is in the front.

Flowers
Basecoat the flowers Ultra White and let dry. Go over petals with a thin wash of Candlelight, leaving an outside edge of the Ultra White showing. Let dry. Use the 1/4" angular brush and shade the petals with Mushroom. Apply tints to the shaded areas one at a time, letting the first tint dry before applying the other. The first tint is Mix #1, Light Peach + Harvest Orange (3:1) the second is Eggplant + Ultra White (1:1). Basecoat the centers Maize. Shade PermEnamel Raw Sienna at the base of the center. Let dry. Apply a second shade of Raw Sienna + Chocolate (1:1). Highlight the centers with Maize + a touch of Ultra White. Apply dots with Chocolate.

Stems and Branches
With the #10/0 liner brush, basecoat the stems and branches with PermEnamel Burnt Sienna. On the finer branches, use some Thinner with the paint. Shade with Chocolate.

Raspberries
Apply Country Tomato to the dark area (on the left side and top of the berry) with the 1/8" angular brush, and pat-blend the rest of the berry with Mix #1. Let dry. Using the #20/0 Ultra Mini Script, form the cells by applying circles on the berries with thinned Ultra White. Let dry.

Using the 1/8" angular brush, wash a bit of Eggplant + a touch of Ultra White in the darkest area of the berry and Country Tomato over the rest (just enough to tint the Ultra White circles). Add a touch of Chocolate to separate the berries, and tint the darker areas a bit at the top of the darker berries. Wash a highlight on some of the cells with Mix #1 + a touch of Ultra White added. Add Ultra White highlight dots on some of the cells.

Leaves
Basecoat all the leaves (except the berry leaves) with the following:
Mix #3: Olive + Latte + Ultra White (2:2:1). Let dry.

The following mixes are used for shading and highlighting:
1st shade: Mix #3 + Hunter Green (2:1)
2nd shade: Hunter Green with just a touch of Mix #3
3rd shade: Hunter Green in the V areas
Highlight: Latte with a touch of Mix #3
Add a wash of Eggplant + Country Tomato (1:1) in the deepest shade areas. Add tints of Country Tomato here and there.

Basecoat the little berry leaves with Mix #3 + Hunter Green (2:1). Apply the same second and third shades and highlight as the other leaves.

Clock Circle and Serving Tray Tile Border
Float the shade on the inside edge with PermEnamel Burnt Sienna and glazing medium mix. Use thin applications, and pity-pat color out for a soft look.

Numbers, Lettering, and Tendrils
Using the #2 round brush, basecoat with PermEnamel Burnt Sienna that has been weakened with Thinner. Shade with Chocolate.

Floral Design on Outside Edges of Clock
With the #10/0 liner brush, outline the design with thinned Burnt Sienna. Using the 1/4" angular brush shade the design with Burnt Sienna and glazing medium mix.

Finishing
Apply two coats of Satin Glaze (plus a couple drops of Thinner added) to the surface, letting each application dry well between coats.

Peach Serving Tray
Sand lightly and remove dust with a tack cloth.
Refer to Staining in General Instructions.
Transfer pattern with white transfer paper.

The wood tray is painted with Delta Ceramcoat paints. All shading is done with soft floats of color. I also use a touch of Gel Blending Medium on my brush along with the paint for the glazes.

Flowers
Basecoat the flowers with Ivory. The centers are based in Straw. With the 1/4" angular brush, apply the first shade in the center with Raw Sienna. The second shade is Burnt Umber. Shade the petals with Light Ivory + a touch of Persimmon. Apply a thin wash of Candy Bar Brown + a touch of Gel Blending Medium to strengthen. Highlight the edges of the petals with Light Ivory. The dots in the centers are Light Ivory + a touch of Straw. The dark dots are Dark Chocolate.

Leaves
Basecoat all the leaves with Wedgwood Green. Shade with Dark Foliage Green + a touch of Wedgwood Green. Wash the shaded area with Candy Bar Brown. Highlight the leaves with Wedgwood Green + a touch of Light Ivory.

Peaches

Flowers, done in four stages.

Leaf Step #1   Step #2   Step #3

Color Mixes #1 #2 #3

Branches
Using the #2 round brush, basecoat the branches first with Ceramcoat Burnt Sienna, then stroke over them with Dark Chocolate.

Raspberries
With the #20/0 Ultra Mini Script, outline the berry cells with Ivory. Using the 1/8" angular brush, pat-blend (having a touch of Gel Blending Medium on the brush), starting with the darkest color to the lightest with Barn Red, Napthol Crimson, and Persimmon. The cells' outline should still show through. Shade lightly with Candy Bar Brown + a touch of Gel Blending Medium. Highlight dots are Light Ivory in the middle area of the berry and Light Ivory + a touch of Persimmon in the outer areas.

Antiquing
Before antiquing, spray surface lightly with Krylon 1311 Matte Finish Spray, so the antiquing will not be too dark. Apply stain over the design and wipe off with a clean, soft cloth. Darken the corners and edges a bit, and fade out.

Finishing
Spray several light coats of Blair Satin Tole Finish.

Peach Clock Frame
Sand lightly and wipe with a tack cloth.
Stain the frame. Refer to Staining in General Instructions.
Basecoat the inner green edge with Dark Foliage Green + Black Green (1:1). Base the gold area with Metallic Kim Gold + Burnt Umber. (2:1)

Antiquing
Antique with the stain in the same manner as the tray.

Finishing
Spray several light coats of Blair Satin Tole Finish.

Peaches Floral on Small Bowl

Palette

Delta Air-Dry PermEnamel
14K Gold
Candlelight
Chocolate
Harvest Orange
Hunter Green
Latte
Light Burgundy
Light Peach
Maize
Mushroom
Olive
Raw Sienna
Ultra White
Air-Dry PermEnamel Clear Gloss Glaze
Air-Dry PermEnamel Retarder
Air-Dry PermEnamel Satin Glaze
Air-Dry PermEnamel Surface Conditioner
Air-Dry PermEnamel Thinner

Brushes

Silver Brush Limited
Golden Natural Series 2006S 1/8", 1/4" Angular
Ultra Mini Series 2407S #20/0 Script
Ruby Satin Series 2503S #2 Filbert
Silver Wee Mop Series 5319S 1/8"
Crystal Series 6807S #10/0 Script Liner

Supplies

Glass bowl with lid, Item #18-7628, available from Viking Woodcrafts, Inc.
Porcelain Disk 3 3/4" round, available from Gold Seal Products
Grey transfer paper
A piece of household sponge
E-6000 adhesive
Bubble palette used with palette paper

Instructions

Lid
The wooden lid is stained. Please read General Instructions for Staining.

Porcelain Disk
Prepare the disk as per General Instructions under Porcelain. Transfer pattern lightly with grey transfer paper. The medium used with the paint is Retarder. Be sure each application of paint is dry before applying another.

Flower Petals
Load the brush with Retarder and then wipe lightly on a paper towel before picking up the paint on the brush. Blend on the palette paper. Using the #2 filbert brush, base the petals of the flowers with Candlelight. Using the 1/4" angular brush, float the shade on the petals with Mushroom. Add tints of Ultra White + Harvest Orange + Latte (2:1:1), in the shaded areas. Add another tint of Light Burgundy in the darkest part of the shaded areas. Highlight the edges of the petals with Ultra White.

Flower Centers
Base with Maize. Shade the base of the center with Raw Sienna. Apply a second shade of Raw Sienna + Chocolate (1:1), only do not extend this shade up as far as the first. Highlight the tops of the centers with Maize + a touch of Ultra White added. The dots around the centers are Chocolate.

Leaves
Using your 1/4" angular brush for the large leaves and your 1/8" angular for the small leaves, base-tint the leaves with Olive + Latte (1:1). Use the #10/0 liner to paint the stems. With the same mix thinned down a bit with a little Thinner + a touch of Retarder, apply vein lines with the #20/0 script liner brush. Shade the base and tip of the leaf with the same base-tint mix. On the large leaves, apply a second shade at the base of the leaves with Hunter Green + base-tint mix (1:1). Tint all the leaves in the V areas with Raw Sienna + Chocolate (1:1). Add tints on the stems of Raw Sienna + a touch of Chocolate, thinned down.

Background
Using the 1/4" angular brush, float-shade around the design with thinned Raw Sienna + a touch of Chocolate. As you are floating the shade around the design, do a little at a time, and buff out the edges of the float with the 1/8" Wee Mop brush.

Disk Finishing
Apply 14K Gold around the edge of the disk.
Finish by applying a coat of Satin Glaze, with a drop of Thinner added, over the entire disk.
Attach the disk to the lid with E-6000 adhesive.

Glass Bowl
Wash and dry the bowl. Brush on the Surface Conditioner and let dry. Dampen a piece of household sponge (about 1" square) with water. Pat all the water out of it as best as you can with a paper towel. Apply a little Retarder to the sponge and then some Light Peach. Tap on the palette till you see all the little holes in the sponge. Tap lightly all over the outside of the bowl. This gives a lacy effect. Let dry. On the top and bottom rims, tap 14K Gold. Let dry.

Finishing
Apply a coat of Clear Gloss Glaze over the entire outside of the bowl.

15

Strawberries and Blueberries Metal Bowl

Palette
Delta Air-Dry PermEnamel
Chocolate
Classic Navy Blue
Dark Goldenrod
Harvest Orange
Hunter Green
Light Burgundy
Olive
Purple
Red Iron Oxide
Ultra Black
Ultra White
Air-Dry PermEnamel Retarder
Air-Dry PermEnamel Satin Glaze
Air-Dry PermEnamel Surface Conditioner
Air-Dry PermEnamel Thinner

Brushes
Silver Brush Limited
Golden Natural Series 2000S #2 Round
Golden Natural Series 2003S #4, 6 Filbert
Golden Natural Series 2006S 1/8", 1/4" Angular
Golden Natural Series 2008S 3/4" Square Wash

Supplies
Shallow metal bowl, Item #129-0016, available from Viking Woodcrafts, Inc.
Bubble palette used with palette paper
Chalk Pencil
Plastic wrap or plastic freezer bag for faux-finishing
White transfer paper
Foam plate

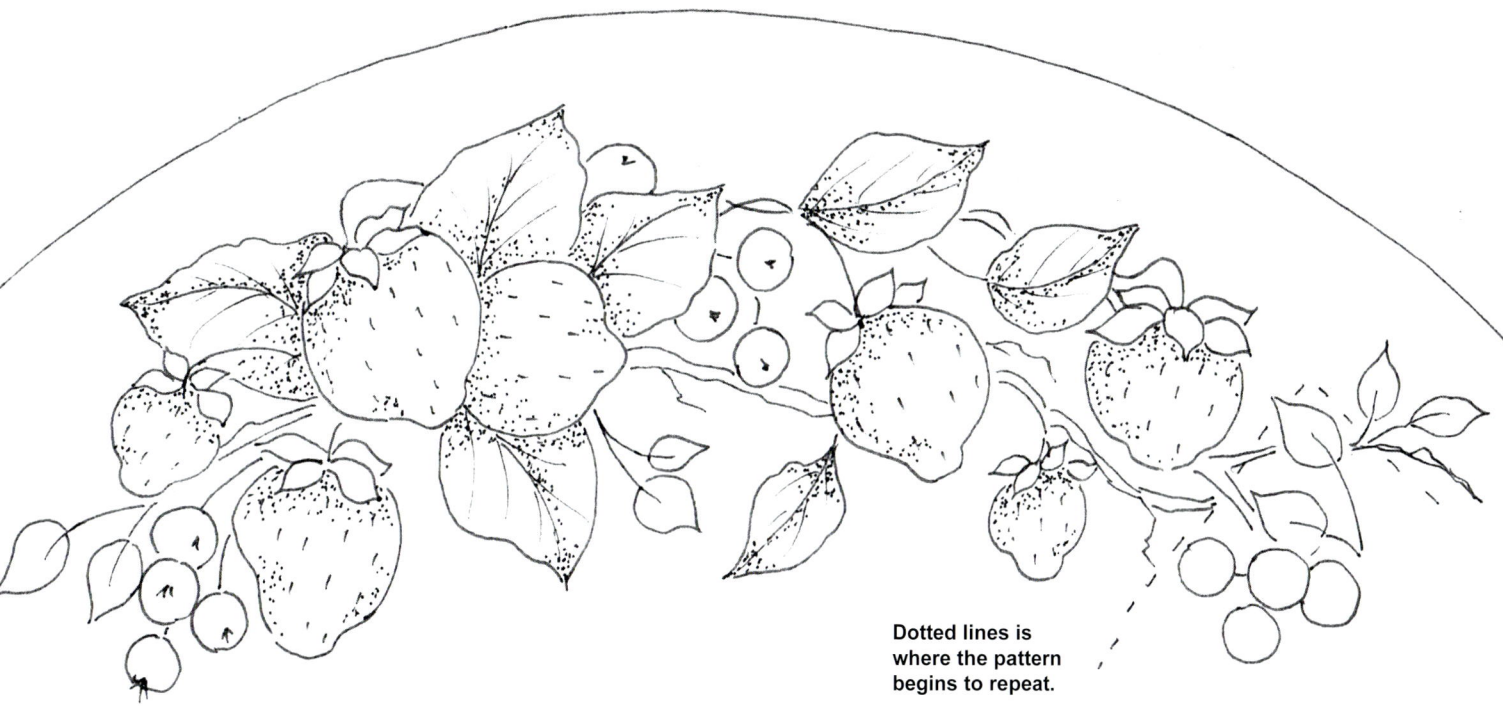

Dotted lines is where the pattern begins to repeat.

Instructions
Please read General Instructions. The medium used along with the paint is Retarder.

Brush on Surface Conditioner. Let Dry.
With the 3/4" wash brush, basecoat the plate Hunter Green + Ultra White (3:1) front and back. Let dry.

Faux-finishing
I use a plastic freezer bag, and it works great! Using the base mix add more Ultra White to it (3:2) and lots of Retarder. On a foam plate, mix the paint with some Retarder in it, and pour some Retarder next to it, in case you need more. Crumple up the plastic wrap or bag and pick up some of the paint and Retarder on it. Tap it on a piece of palette paper so you don't get a glob on the surface of the piece. As you faux-finish the bowl, leave some of the background showing. Work on one side, let dry, and then work on the other.

Measure in a 1/4" band, and mark off with a chalk pencil. I used a compass for this: Hold the compass to the outside edge as you turn the bowl. Base the band Hunter Green. Transfer the pattern with white transfer paper.

Basecoat the following using the filbert brushes #4 and #6.
Mix 1, Leaves: Hunter Green + Olive + Ultra White (1:1: t).
Blueberries: Ultra White + a touch of Classic Navy Blue
Strawberries: One dime-size puddle of Ultra White + two drops of Dark Goldenrod.
Branches: Mix #1 + a touch of Chocolate added (makes a Muddy Greenish Brown).

Leaves
Brushes used for shading are the 1/8" and 1/4" angular. Shade the base of the leaf and the tips with Hunter Green. Let dry. Apply the vein lines with the #10/0 liner and Hunter Green, keeping it thin. Let dry. Re-shade the leaves, beginning by floating in the center vein line. Let dry, then shade the base of the leaf and the tip again. In the V areas shade again with Hunter Green + Purple (2:1). The tints on the leaves are added later. There are no tints on the little berry leaves.

Blueberries
Using the 1/8" angular brush, base-tint around each berry with Classic Navy Blue + a touch of Ultra Black added. Let dry. Lightly add tints of Harvest Orange + Purple (1:1), on only one side of the berry. The center pod areas are Hunter Green + Purple (2:1), applied with the #10/0 liner brush. Outline the center with short strokes of Ultra White.

Strawberries
The shading and base-tinting are done with the 1/4" angular brush. There are many shades on the berries, because each shade is a very transparent shade, building up depth. (See pattern for shading placement.)

The first shade is done with a dime-size puddle of Ultra White + four drops of Harvest Orange. Let dry. Base-tint all around the berry except the right side (keep it thin) with Harvest Orange. If you see a harsh line where you left off, pat-blend some of the first shade into it. Using the #20/0 Ultra Mini Script, make small, fine dashes in the berries with Ultra Black. Dot the tops of these with Ultra White. Let dry. Wash over the berries with thin Red Iron Oxide and Retarder. Shade the berries again with Red Iron Oxide. Let dry. Apply another shade with Light Burgundy. I shaded some only in the dark area, and some I base-tinted all around the berry, for a variety. In the V areas of the berry, shade with Light Burgundy + a touch of Hunter Green added.

Branches
Shade the branches with Chocolate, using the 1/8" angular brush. Highlight with a few streaks of Dark Goldenrod + Harvest Orange (1:1). With this same color, add tints on some of the leaves. On a few areas of the branches and the larger leaves, add a few tints of Red Iron Oxide.

Finishing
With the 3/4" wash brush, apply at least two coats of Satin Glaze thinned down with a drop or two of Thinner.

Strawberries & Blueberries on Glass Bowl with Lid

Palette
Delta Air-Dry PermEnamel, used on porcelain disk
Harvest Orange
Hunter Green
Light Burgundy
Midnight
Raw Sienna
Red Iron Oxide
Ultra Black
Ultra White
Air-Dry PermEnamel Retarder
Air-Dry PermEnamel Satin Glaze
Air-Dry PermEnamel Surface Conditioner
Air-Dry PermEnamel Thinner

Delta Ceramcoat, used on wood
Delta All-Purpose Sealer
Rainforest Green
White

Brushes
Silver Brush Limited
Golden Natural Series 2003S #8 Filbert
Golden Natural Series 2006S 1/8", 1/4" Angular
Golden Natural Series 2008S 3/4" Square Wash
Ultra Mini Series 2407S #20/0 Script
Silver Wee Mop Series 5319S 1/8"
Crystal Series 6807S #10/0 Script Liner

Supplies
Glass bowl with lid, Item #18-7628, available from Viking Woodcrafts, Inc.
Porcelain Disk 3 3/4" round, available from Gold Seal Products
Bubble palette used with palette paper
Grey transfer paper
Plastic wrap or plastic freezer bag for faux-finishing
Blair Satin Tole Finish
Tack cloth

Color Mixes
Refer to page 5 for color mix reference.

Instructions for the wooden lid
Sand lightly and wipe with a tack cloth. Seal the wooden lid, and sand lightly and wipe with the tack cloth again. Basecoat the lid with two coats of Rainforest Green. Let dry. Using a foam plate as your palette, apply Rainforest Green + White (3:1) and a little water to thin it down. Faux-finish the lid with a crumpled up piece of plastic wrap or bag. Before you apply the paint to the surface, tap it a few times on a piece of palette paper so you do not get any globs on your surface. Leave some of your background color showing.

Finishing
Spray with Blair Satin Tole Finish.

Porcelain Disk
Please read General Instructions for preparation. The medium used along with the PermEnamel paint is Retarder.

Strawberries
The shading and base-tinting are done with the 1/4" angular brush. There are many shades on the berries, because each shade is a very transparent shade, building up depth. (See pattern for shading placement.)

The first shade is done with a dime-size puddle of Ultra White + four drops of Harvest Orange. Let dry. Base-tint all around the berry except the right side (keep it thin) with Harvest Orange. If you see a harsh line where you left off, pat-blend some of the first shade into it. Using the #20/0 Ultra Mini Script, make small, fine dashes in the berries with Ultra Black. Dot the tops of these with Ultra White. Let dry. Wash over the berries with thin Red Iron Oxide and Retarder. Shade the berries again with Red Iron Oxide. Let dry. Apply another shade with Light Burgundy. I shaded some only in the dark area, and some I base-tinted all around the berry, for a variety. In the V areas of the berry, shade with Light Burgundy + a touch of Hunter Green added.

Blueberries
Base each berry with Midnight plus a touch of Ultra White added. Let dry. Base-tint around each berry using the 1/8" angular brush and Midnight. The dark centers are Midnight. Outline the dark centers with short strokes of Ultra White.

Large Leaves
Base-tint the leaves with Hunter Green + Ultra White (3:1). Let dry. Base-tint in the center vein line. Using the #20/0 script brush, apply small vein lines. Shade the base and the tip of each leaf with Hunter Green + a touch of Midnight. Apply tints of Raw Sienna.

Small Leaves and Strawberry Leaves
Base with Hunter Green + Ultra White (3:1). Shade the leaves with Hunter Green. Using the #10/0 liner brush, base the stems first with Raw Sienna, then go over them with Hunter Green + Ultra White (3:1). Float-tint around design with Hunter Green + Ultra White + Retarder, keeping this very light. Buff out the edges of the float with the 1/8" Wee Mop brush.

Finishing
Apply a coat of Satin Glaze + a drop of Thinner over the disk. Attach the disk to the lid with E-6000 adhesive.

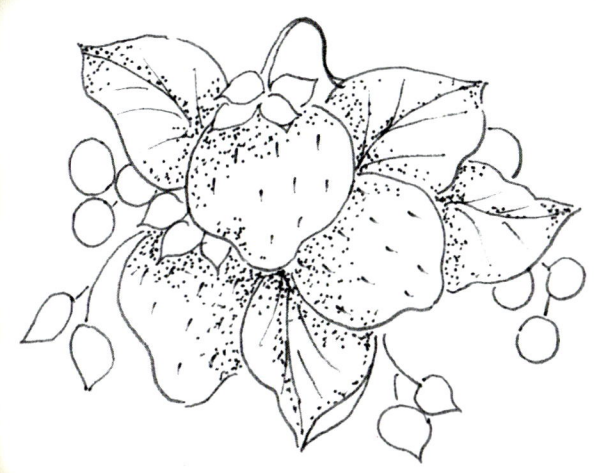

Line drawing 100% scale.

Country Canisters and Lotion Dispenser

Palette
Delta Air-Dry PermEnamel
Burnt Sienna
Chocolate
Dark Goldenrod
Harvest Orange
Hunter Green
Light Blue
Light Peach
Marshmallow
Olive
Raw Sienna
Royal Purple
Tropical Purple
Ultra Black
Ultra White
Air-Dry PermEnamel Retarder
Air-Dry PermEnamel Satin Glaze
Air-Dry PermEnamel Surface Conditioner
Air-Dry PermEnamel Thinner

Brushes
Silver Brush Limited
Golden Natural Series 2000S #2 Round
Golden Natural Series 2002S #2 Bright
Golden Natural Series 2003S #6, #8 Filbert
Golden Natural Series 2006S 1/4", 1/2" Angular
Golden Natural Series 2008S 3/4" Square Wash
Ultra Mini Series 2407S #20/0 Script
Ruby Satin Series 2503S #2 Filbert
Silver Wee Mop Series 5319S 1/8"

Supplies
Canisters, Item numbers #C902L, #C902M, #C902S, available from Rynne China Company
Lotion Dispenser, Item #186-0001, available from Viking Woodcrafts, Inc.
Bubble palette used with palette paper
A small piece of household sponge

Color Mixes
Refer to page 5 for color mix reference.

Instructions
Please read General Instructions under China.

Clean the surface, and brush on Surface Conditioner to the canisters (bottom scenery area only) with the 3/4" wash brush. Let dry. Apply a coat of Satin Glaze (with a couple of drops of Thinner added) to the scenery portion of the canisters only. I pour about four tablespoons into a small glass dish, about the size of a mayonnaise jar lid, and add two drops of Thinner to it. This is also applied to the lotion dispenser. The tops of the canisters and lids are done last. Apply their Surface Conditioner when you are ready to paint them.

Transfer pattern, omitting the large tree on the front of the large canister. This will be done later. Keep the transferring light.

Sky
Using the 1/2" angular brush, float tints of Light Blue + Ultra White (2:1) on the horizon line and work up a bit. Keep this light and wispy. Do the same at the top, working down a bit. Streak a little through the center. When dry, apply tints of Light Peach right over

21

some of the blue areas on the horizon line and work up a bit. Streak through the center a bit also. Let dry. Strengthen the Light Peach area, where the deepest crevices of the mountains are shaded with a tint of Harvest Orange + Ultra White (1:1).

Mountains
With the #6 filbert, basecoat the mountains with Hunter Green + Royal Purple + Ultra White (2:1:2), keeping them light. Add tints of Tropical Purple here and there to give some variation.

Ground
Use the 1/4" angular brush for most of these applications of color. For the larger areas I used a #8 filbert brush. There are many applications of color in the ground area. It is best to do the first application of color for placement's sake and then proceed to the background trees and all the bushes. The first application of color is Hunter Green + Ultra White (1:1). This is applied like a wash of color, not heavy. There are many tints, building up slowly. Keep it light.

The tints are:
Olive + Ultra White (1:1/2)
Hunter Green + Olive + Ultra White (1:1:t)
Hunter Green + Ultra White (3:1)
Olive + Raw Sienna (1:1)
I also tap some of these tints in.

Background Trees and Bushes
Use the 1/8" Wee Mop and stipple in the background trees and all of the bushes with Hunter Green + Royal Purple + a touch of Ultra White (3:1:t).

The first higlight is Hunter Green + Olive + a touch of Ultra White (1:1:t). The second is Olive + Ultra White (1:1). On some of the background trees near the mountains, stipple Hunter Green + Ultra White (3:1) to add some variation.

Afterward, on some of the bushes, stipple some Royal Purple + Ultra White and Harvest Orange + Ultra White, then highlight with more Ultra White added. Because some of the flowers are so small, use this method to apply the highlights: Load the 1/8" Wee Mop brush with the mix, tip one side of the edge of the brush into the Ultra White, pat once on the palette, then apply the highlights to the flowers.

Barn and Silo
Grey Mixes
Light Grey: Ultra Black + Ultra White (1:3)
Medium Grey: Ultra Black + Ultra White (2:1)
Dark Grey: Ultra Black + Ultra White (4:1)

Basecoat the roof of the barn with the Dark Grey Mix. Highlight the roof with Burnt Sienna. Apply a second highlight of Burnt Sienna + a touch of Dark Goldenrod. With the background color of the china as the basecoat, shade the barn and silo with the Light Grey Mix. Use the #20/0 Ultra Mini Script and pull down some lines indicating barn boards with the Light Grey Mix also. Add tints of Tropical Purple on the upper right side in the shade area under the roof of the barn. Add tints of Burnt Sienna in the shaded areas near the bottom. The lines on the silo are the Medium Grey Mix. The inside of the barn door, beginning at the top, is Chocolate. Then add some Burnt Sienna toward the center, and at the bottom work in some Light Peach with the Burnt Sienna, extending into the path area. The stalls are put in with the Medium Grey Mix and highlighted with the Light Grey Mix. When dry, shade the top right again with Chocolate, extending over the posts lightly. Float a shade at the bottom of the stalls, extending out into the pathway a bit inside of the barn. The hinges on the barn doors are the Dark Grey Mix. Highlight the top edges of the barn doors with the Light Grey Mix. Add the X on the doors first with the Light Grey Mix, then shade with the Dark Grey Mix. There is a little hay on the floor inside of the barn, and this is done with the #20/0 script and Dark Goldenrod, highlighted with a little Ultra White added. Using the #2 flat shader, basecoat the window and other barn opening with Burnt Sienna, and shade them with Chocolate. The window frame and small door frame are Ultra White. Also, the edge of the roof is done in Ultra White. Add tints of Light Peach on the highlighted area of the barn and center right of the silo.

Large Tree and Bare Trees
After the grass and the barn are completed, transfer the large tree. Use the #2 Ruby Satin Filbert and basecoat the trunk and stems with the Medium Grey Mix. With the 1/4" angular brush, shade with Chocolate. Add a few highlights with the Light Grey Mix. Add tints of Harvest Orange + Ultra White on the highlights on the right side of the tree. The tree foliage is first stippled in with Hunter Green + Olive + a touch of Ultra White. Highlight with Olive + Ultra White, and then add a bit more Ultra White for a final highlight on the right side.

The bare trees scattered through the design are Chocolate. The limb on the small canister is done the same way as the large tree, except without the orange tint.

Paths
There are two different paths: the main paths on the front of the canisters that extend to the sides and one on the back of the large canister. First, the main ones. The background color of the china is used as the basecoat. With the 1/4" angular brush, float tints of color onto the paths, then work some of that color into the ground areas near the flowers. Start by the edge of the grass, and tap out into the path. The tints are as follows: Burnt Sienna with a touch of Ultra White, Light Blue, Tropical Purple, Light Peach, and just a touch of Harvest Orange + Ultra White (1:1). The tints are all very lightly patted in. Also add some of the greens and tints of Olive + Raw Sienna.

The path on the back is painted after the greens are painted in. Using the #6 filbert brush, lay in the path with Light Peach. Add some tints of Burnt Sienna + Ultra White. The edges of the path are tints of Olive + Raw Sienna. Apply some of this color on the ground in front of the larger tree in the back. The stones are Chocolate + a touch of Ultra White added.

Grasses
Using the #20/0 Ultra Mini Script, pull up the grasses. The colors are Olive + Ultra White and Olive + Raw Sienna.

Geese
Here again the background color of the china is the basecoat. With the 1/4" angular brush, base-tint the dark goose with the Medium Grey Mix. With the background as the highlight, deepen shading with the Dark Grey Mix. Add touches of Marshmallow in the highlight area. Add tints of Burnt Sienna in the V shaded areas.

The white goose is shaded with the Light Grey Mix. Add touches of Raw Sienna in the shade areas. Add Marshmallow in the highlight areas.

Timeless Treasures
with PermEnamel

The spirit of man is the candle of the Lord,..

Pro. 20:27

Collar

Repeat Design

Angel T-Light page 27

All patterns are 2006© by **Sharon Shannon**

Country Canisters and Lotion Dispenser pages 20-23

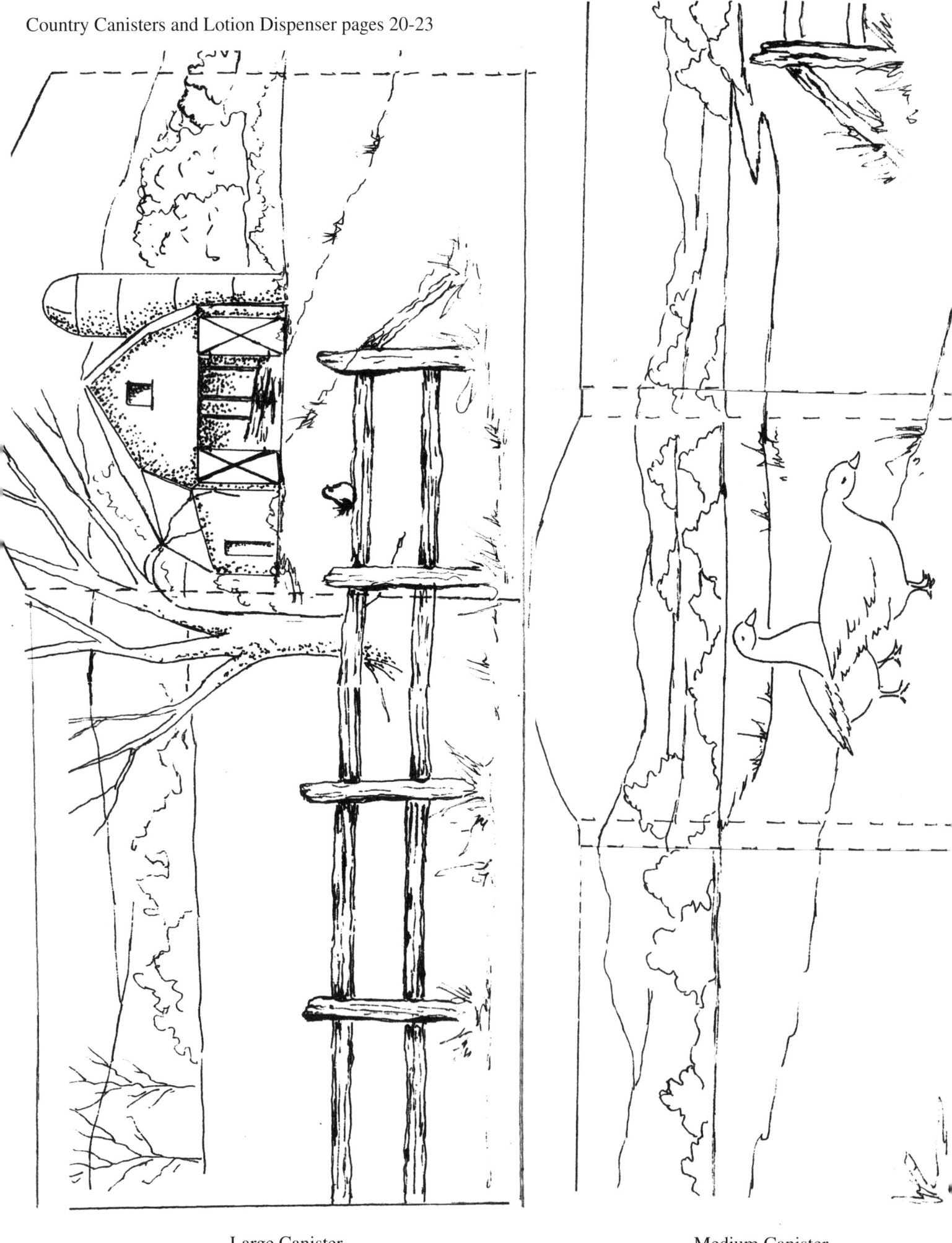

Large Canister

Medium Canister

Winter's Glory pages 25-26

Serenity
pages 40-43

Bottom Left
Serenity

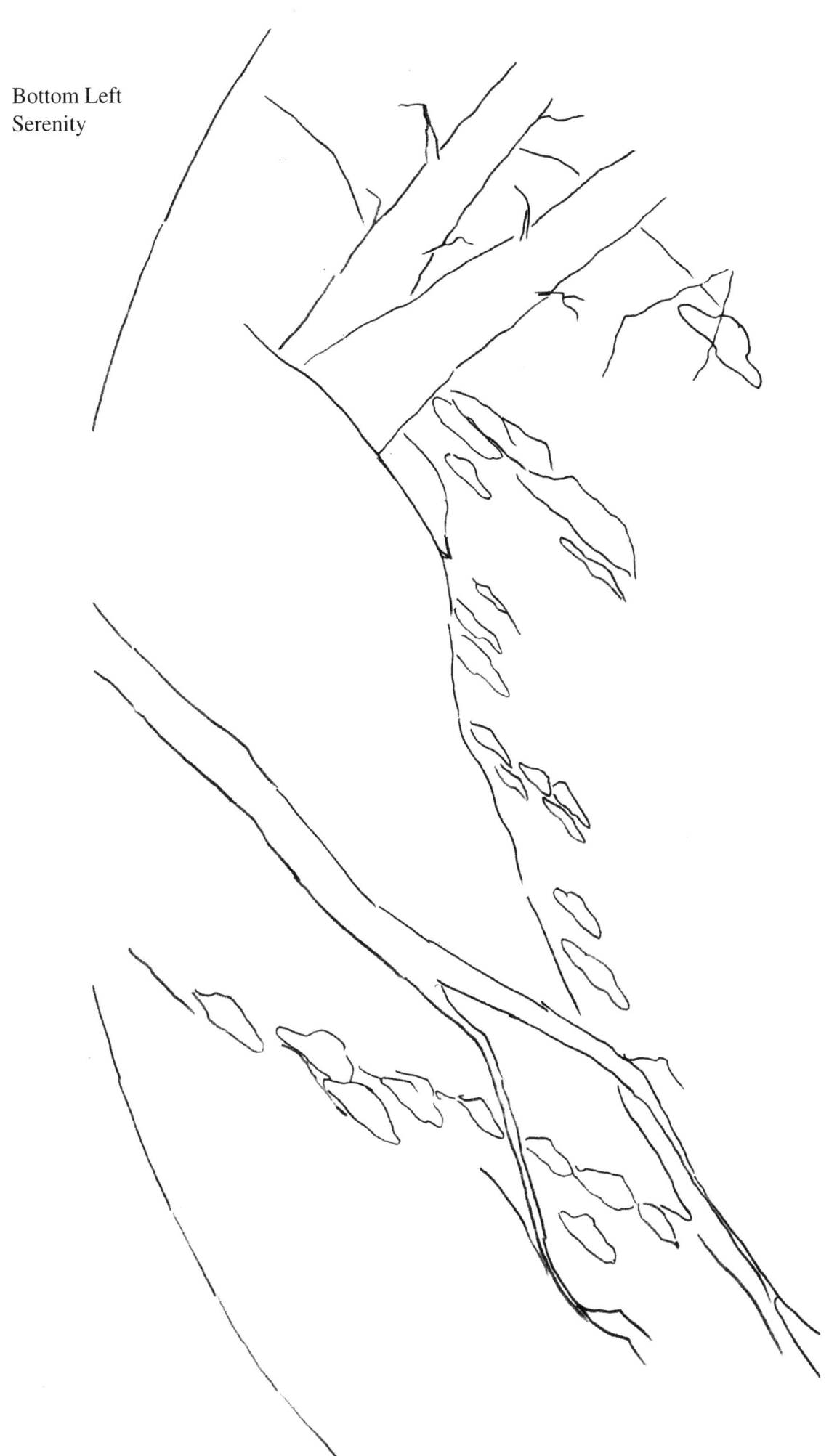

Top Left
Serenity

Top Right
Serenity

Broken lines are for Pine Trees.

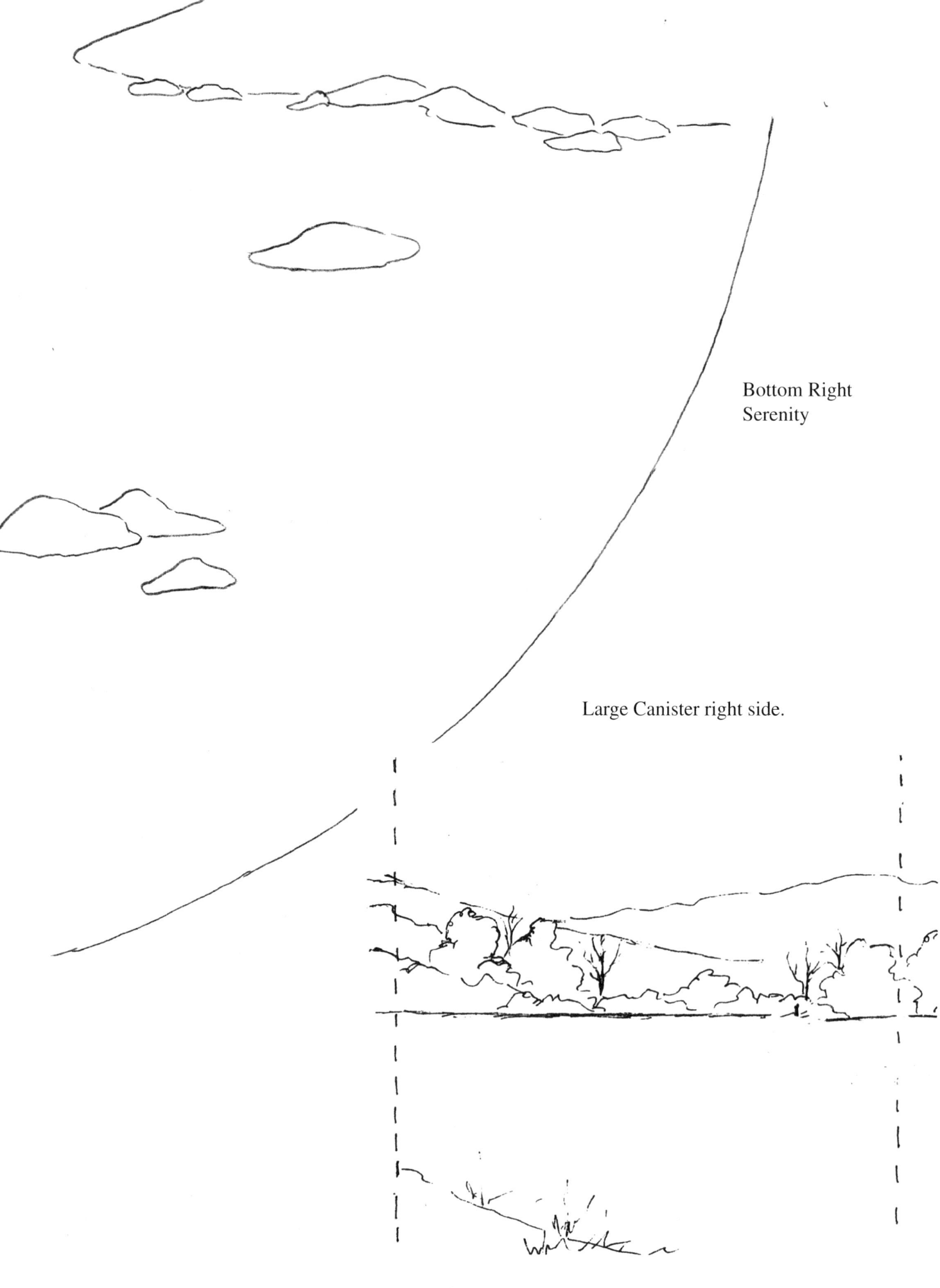

With the #20/0 Ultra Mini Script, base the eyes black and apply a white highlight. The beaks and feet are Harvest Orange with a touch of white added. Highlight them with Dark Goldenrod. Shade the beaks near the faces with Burnt Sienna. Pull out some feathers over the top of the geese's legs to pull the legs into the body.

Add tints of Chocolate with a touch of Ultra White added under their feet. Just tap them in, simulating some rough dirt.

Fences
Basecoat the fences with the Medium Grey Mix. Shade with Chocolate. Highlight with the Light Grey Mix. The second highlights are touches of Ultra White. Add some Chocolate grain lines and highlight with a few Ultra White lines here and there. The rope on the fence (on the small canister) is Chocolate.

Flowers Near the Fences
With the 1/8" Wee Mop, stipple in the flowers by the fences. They are Royal Purple + Ultra White and Harvest Orange + Ultra White. There are also some little Ultra White ones and a few little dots of Dark Goldenrod. Pat some of these tint colors into the ground area near the fences also.

Birds
With the #2 round brush, basecoat the birds with the Medium Grey Mix. Their stomachs are stroked in Ultra White. Use the #20/0 Ultra Mini Script for the tail feathers. First load the brush with the Dark Grey Mix, and then touch the tip of the brush into Ultra White. Pull strokes from the end of the feather into the body of the bird. Reload the brush in the same way for each feather. The birds' eyes are Ultra Black with an Ultra White highlight. Their beaks and feet are Dark Goldenrod.

Tops of Canisters and Lids
Brush on Surface Conditioner and let dry. Take a small piece of household sponge, and dampen with water to soften. Wring all the water out. With Retarder and the mountains' basecoat mix, sponge lightly on surfaces.

Finishing
Apply at least two coats of Satin Glaze, with a couple of drops of Thinner added, over entire canisters.

Lotion Dispenser

Remaining canister line drawings can be found in the pull-out pattern pages in the center of this book.

Small Canister

23

Winter's Glory

Palette
Delta Air-Dry PermEnamel
Chocolate
Classic Navy Blue
Hunter Green
Marshmallow
Red Iron Oxide
Ultra Black
Ultra White
Air-Dry PermEnamel Retarder
Air-Dry PermEnamel Satin Glaze
Air-Dry PermEnamel Surface Conditioner
Air-Dry PermEnamel Thinner

Brushes
Silver Brush Limited
Golden Natural Series 2002S #2 Shader
Golden Natural Series 2003S #6, #8 Filbert
Golden Natural Series 2006S 1/8", 1/4" Angular
Golden Natural Series 2008S 3/4" Square Wash
Crystal Series 6807S #10/0 Script Liner
Silver Wee Mop Series 5319S 1/8"

Supplies
This winter scene was done on a white tin pocket I had, but painting can be done on any white tin or white enamel piece of your choice.
Bubble palette used with palette paper
Grey transfer paper
Cosmetic sponge

Instructions
Brush on Surface Conditioner with the 3/4" wash brush. Let dry. Basecoat the surface with Marshmallow by pat-blending with a cosmetic sponge + a bit of Retarder. This technique may sound unusual, but it works well. Let dry. Transfer the pattern lightly with grey transfer paper.

Tinting the Sky
When you load the brush with the tint color, wipe most of it off on a paper towel, then pick up Retarder on the brush and work the remaining color on the palette. There should be just a hint of color left on the brush. Using the #8 filbert brush, tint the sky just a little here and there with Marshmallow + a very little touch of Classic Navy Blue, keeping it light. Add tints of Red Iron Oxide + Chocolate + Ultra White (2:1:1) very lightly near the horizon line and a little on the upper right side. Then go over it with Marshmallow to soften and blend.

Grey Mixes
Light Grey: Ultra Black + Ultra White (1:3)
Medium Grey: Ultra Black + Ultra White (2:1)
Dark Grey: Ultra Black + Ultra White (4:1)

Background Trees
Using the 1/8" Wee Mop, tap in the background trees with the Light Grey Mix. Tap in a little Chocolate + Ultra White here and there. Tap in Marshmallow on the tops of the trees.

Ground Shading
Use the 1/4" angular brush and also the #6 filbert brush. The angular is good when you are floating a tint near a building or area, and the filbert is good for brushing hints of color on large snow areas. Tint the ground in the shaded areas with the Light Grey Mix. Add tints of Chocolate + Marshmallow (2:1) in the pathways. Apply tints of Marshmallow + a touch of Classic Navy Blue + a touch of Hunter Green (a very light bluish-green color) on the snow here and there and also in the paths. You will not need much of this. Keep it light. If it gets too overpowering, go over with Marshmallow.

25

Barns

Basecoat the barn with Red Iron Oxide + Chocolate (2:1). The barn is shaded with Chocolate. Let dry. The highlight is the base color + more Ultra White added (2:1). Apply a second shade in the V areas with the barn base color with a touch of Ultra Black added. The windows are the Dark Grey Mix, done with the #2 flat shader. Using the #10/0 liner brush, outline the windows and door frames with Chocolate + Marshmallow (2:1). Apply very fine vertical streaks of the Light Grey Mix with the liner brush.

Barn Roofs

The background color is the color of the roofs of the barns. They are shaded and then gone over with Marshmallow. Using the 1/4" angular brush, shade from the bottom of the roof up with the Medium Grey Mix, pat-blending as you go. Now work down from the top with Marshmallow and go over the shade a bit to soften. The chimney is the barn base color, shaded with a touch of Ultra Black added. With Marshmallow, add a little snow on the ledges of the windows and door frames and on top of the chimney.

Silo

Base the silo in the Medium Grey Mix. Highlight with the Light Grey Mix, and shade with the Dark Grey Mix. Tap some snow on the top with Marshmallow.

Sled

Basecoat the sled with Chocolate + Marshmallow (3:1). The runners and the top area of the handle are the Dark Grey Mix. Tap on some snow with Marshmallow.

Fences

The fences are based in Chocolate + Marshmallow (3:1). Shade with a little of the Dark Grey Mix. Tap on some snow with Marshmallow.

Bare Trees

Base the trees with Chocolate + Marshmallow (2:1). Add touches of the Dark Grey Mix on the right side of the trunks and a bit on the branches. Highlight with Marshmallow snow here and there.

Pine Trees

Using the 1/4" angular brush, tap in the center trunk line with Chocolate using the chisel edge of the brush. Using the 1/4" angular or the 1/8" angular brush, tap in the branches, keeping the brush horizontal, with Hunter Green + Classic Navy Blue (3:1). After you have the branches, tap in some Chocolate in the center area of the tree here and there. Tap in the snow on the branches with Marshmallow. Let dry. Tap in more Marshmallow here and there to highlight a few branches on the left side of the tree.

Bottom Branches and Berries

The tint at the bottom is the same tint as in the sky. The bottom branches are done the same way as the bare trees. The berries are the barn base color. Add some snow on the branches and a few of the berries with Marshmallow.

Finishing

Apply two coats of Satin Glaze with a drop or two of Thinner added. Let dry well between coats.

Angel T-Light

Palette
Delta Air-Dry PermEnamel
Harvest Orange
Hunter Green
Light Burgundy
Marshmallow
Raw Sienna
Ultra White
Air-Dry PermEnamel Retarder
Air-Dry PermEnamel Satin Glaze
Air-Dry PermEnamel Surface Conditioner
Air-Dry PermEnamel Thinner

Brushes
Silver Brush Limited
Golden Natural Series 2000S #5/0 Round
Golden Natural Series 2003S #2 Filbert
Golden Natural Series 2006S 1/8" Angular
Ultra Mini Series 2407S #20/0 Script Liner
Crystal Series 6807S #10/0 Script Liner

Supplies
Angel T-Light Item #SU10071, available retail from Quilt Cottage or wholesale from Sunny Gifts (USA), Inc. #SU10071-02-01150-02
Bubble palette used with palette paper
White transfer paper

While I was shopping with my niece Kelly, we came upon this darling little quilt shop. As soon as I walked through the door I spied this cute Angel T-Light. I fell in love with it and knew I wanted to put it into this book. I kept the design simple, to not take away from the charm it has on its own. I hope you enjoy it.

Instructions
Brush on Surface Conditioner. Let dry. There is no basecoating. I left the angel the color it was. Transfer the pattern with white transfer paper. The medium used with the paint is the Retarder.

Lettering
With the #5/0 round brush, apply lettering with Marshmallow.

Pine Boughs
Using the #10/0 script liner brush, stroke in the boughs and stems first with Raw Sienna + Marshmallow (2:1). Leaving some of the Raw Sienna + Marshmallow needles showing, apply more needles with Hunter Green + a touch of Ultra White, then Hunter Green and Ultra White (1:1). Highlight some of them with Ultra White.

Berries
Base the berries with Harvest Orange. This will take two coats. Shade the base of the berry with Light Burgundy. Highlight the tops with Harvest Orange + Ultra White (1:1). Add little Marshmallow shine marks with the liner brush.

Finishing
Apply Satin Glaze with a couple of drops of Thinner added to the entire angel, so the finish will look uniform.

Porcelain Ornament: O Christmas Tree

Palette
Delta Air-Dry PermEnamel
14K Gold
Burnt Sienna
Chocolate
Harvest Orange
Hunter Green
Light Burgundy
Light Peach
Maize
Midnight
Ultra Black
Ultra White
Victorian Rose
Air-Dry PermEnamel Retarder
Air-Dry PermEnamel Satin Glaze
Air-Dry PermEnamel Surface Conditioner
Air-Dry PermEnamel Thinner

Brushes
Silver Brush Limited
Golden Natural Series 2002S #2 Bright
Golden Natural Series 2003S #2 Filbert
Golden Natural Series 2006S 1/8" Angular Golden Natural Series 2008S 3/4" Square Wash
Ultra Mini Series 2407 #20/0 Script
Silver Wee Mop Series 5319S 1/8", 3/8"
Crystal Series 6807S #10/0 Script Liner

Supplies
Porcelain star (#ST-1), available from Gold Seal Products or wood star, item #207-0274 available from Viking Woodcrafts, Inc. (See PermEnamel Color Conversion Chart in General Instructions for painting on wood with Ceramcoat paints.)
Bubble palette used with palette paper
Grey transfer paper

Preparation
See General Instructions.
Wash ornament with soap and water, rinse well, and dry. Apply Surface Conditioner with the 3/4" wash brush and let dry.

Instructions
Transfer pattern lightly with grey transfer paper. Using the liner brush, outline facial features with Light Peach + a touch of Burnt Sienna (to make a Dark Flesh color), plus Retarder on the brush. By doing this you will see her facial details through the basecoat that you will apply on her face. Let dry. With the #2 filbert, go over her face with a thin application of Light Peach. Shade her face with the Dark Flesh Mix. Reapply her eyebrows, nose, and mouth again with the Dark Flesh Mix. Using Burnt Sienna, go over the eye details, and strengthen the center line of her mouth.

Eyes
Darken the iris with Chocolate and add Ultra White highlights. Add a touch of thin Ultra White to her bottom lip.

Cheek
Blush on her cheek is Victorian Rose. Use the 1/8" angular brush, and go over with the 1/8" Wee Mop to soften. If you have a harsh line showing, add some Light Peach to the outside area, and buff in with the Wee Mop.

Clothing
Her hat and coat are base-tinted first with Victorian Rose with the 1/8" angular brush. Let dry. Base-tint again; this time pitty-pat the color in to cover the area and give texture to the clothing. Repeat again for extra coverage. Remember to use light applications of color each time. As you repeat this step don't go over the area that is highlighted. Shade with Light Burgundy. Buttons are Ultra Black with Ultra White highlights.

Her scarf and pompoms on her hat are based Ultra Black + Ultra White (1:3) for a Light Grey color using the #2 Bright brush. Using the #20/0 Ultra Mini Script brush, apply the plaid linework on her scarf with Maize and Victorian Rose. Shade her scarf with a Dark Grey Mix of Ultra Black and Ultra White (4:1). Pull out fringe on the pompoms and scarf with Ultra White, Maize, and the Dark Grey Mix. Her gloves are the Light Grey Mix, shaded with the Dark Grey Mix and highlighted with Ultra White.

Hair
With the #20 Ultra Mini Script brush, pull out wisps of hair with Burnt Sienna. Float a shade under her hat and by her cheek with thinned Burnt Sienna. Let dry. Float a second shade of Chocolate under the hat on the left side and where the hat bends up.

Shading
The shadow tints around her and the background are thin floats of Midnight + a touch of Ultra White. With the 1/8" Wee Mop brush, tap the edges out as you apply them, resulting in a soft blend.

Pine Boughs
Using the #10/0 script liner, apply thin pine boughs of Hunter Green + Midnight + a touch of Ultra White. You will use more Retarder than usual to make thin pine needles. Build them up gradually. Add a touch of thin Burnt Sienna here and there on the main limbs.

Candles
Base the candles Ultra White. The flame is Maize, shaded at the base with Harvest Orange + a touch of Ultra White. Add an Ultra White highlight. Float around the flame with Maize.

Finishing
Mix Satin Glaze about the size of a quarter with a couple drops of Thinner. Apply a coat of this over the ornament with the 3/8" Wee Mop brush.

Apply 14K Gold to the outside edge of the ornament.

Porcelain Ornament: Dressing Up Frosty

Palette
Delta Air-Dry PermEnamel
14K Gold
Burnt Sienna
Chocolate
Harvest Orange
Light Peach
Midnight
Olive
Raw Sienna
Red Iron Oxide
Ultra Black
Ultra White
Air-Dry PermEnamel Retarder
Air-Dry PermEnamel Satin Glaze
Air-Dry PermEnamel Surface Conditioner
Air-Dry PermEnamel Thinner

Brushes
Silver Brush Limited
Golden Natural Series 2002S #2 Bright
Golden Natural Series 2003S #2 Filbert
Golden Natural Series 2006S 1/8", 1/4" Angular
Golden Natural Series 2008S 3/4" Square Wash
Ultra Mini Series 2407S #20/0 Script
Silver Wee Mop Series 5319S 1/8", 3/8"
Crystal Series 6807S #10/0 Script Liner

Supplies
Porcelain star (#ST-1), available from Gold Seal Products or wood star, item #207-0274 available from Viking Woodcrafts, Inc. (See PermEnamel Color Conversion Chart in General Instructions for painting on wood with Ceramcoat paints.)
Bubble palette used with palette paper
Grey transfer paper

Preparation
See General Instructions. Wash ornament with soap and water, rinse well, and dry. Apply Surface Conditioner with the 3/4" wash brush and let dry. Transfer pattern with grey transfer paper.

Instructions
Girl's Coat and Brown Area of her Hat
Using the #2 Filbert, basecoat her coat Raw Sienna + Chocolate (1:1), which is the Burnt Umber Mix. Shade her coat with Chocolate, using the 1/4" angular brush. Using the 1/8" Wee Mop brush, stipple her coat to make a lightly textured effect with the base color + a touch of Ultra White added (makes a Tan color). Let dry. Re-shade with Chocolate, and highlight with Raw Sienna.

The red areas of her scarf, mittens, and hat are based with Red Iron Oxide, using the #2 Bright brush. With the #10/0 Crystal Script Liner, apply thin stripes of Chocolate and Raw Sienna to her hat, and apply thin lines to make the plaid on her scarf. Shade the areas with Red Iron Oxide + a touch of Chocolate. Highlight with Red Iron Oxide + a touch of Harvest Orange + a touch of Ultra White. Using the #20/0 Ultra Mini Script, pull little hairs out on the red area of her hat and scarf with the highlight color.

Face
Using the 1/8" angular brush, basecoat her face Light Peach + a touch of Burnt Sienna (to make a Dark Flesh color). Add a touch of blush to her cheek with the base mix + a touch of Red Iron Oxide added. With the #20/0 Ultra Mini Script, pull out a few eyelashes with Chocolate. With the #10/0 liner, stroke in her hair with the Burnt Umber Mix. Shade her hair near the hat line with floats of Chocolate using your 1/8" angular brush. Pull out a few hairs back across her hat with Raw Sienna + a touch of Ultra White added.

Snowman
The color of the snowman is the porcelain itself. Using the 1/4" angular brush, shade the snowman with Midnight + Raw Sienna + a touch of Ultra White and lots of Retarder to make it thin. As you float the shade, use the 1/8" Wee Mop and tap out the edges to make it look soft. His eyes, nose, and hat are based Ultra Black. Add a little Ultra White highlight in his eyes and on the tip of his nose. His mouth is little short strokes of Ultra Black. Base his pipe Raw Sienna + Chocolate (1:1). Shade the bowl with Chocolate.

Using either the #2 filbert or Bright, basecoat his scarf with Olive. Apply stripes with Red Iron Oxide and the #10/0 Crystal Script Liner. Let dry. Highlight the tops of the stripes with Raw Sienna. Shade the scarf with Midnight + Olive (1:1). His hat band is also based Olive. Shade the band with Olive + Midnight (1:1) at each end. Highlight the center with Olive + a touch of Ultra White added.

Background
The ground area and around the snowman are thin floats of Midnight + Ultra White. The trees are Olive + Midnight (1:1). Add a little Ultra White to the mix, and highlight here and there.

Pine Boughs
With the #10/0 liner, stroke in the pine needles with Olive, and add some Olive + Midnight needles here and there. Add a touch of Raw Sienna to the main bough line.

Snowman's Broom
Using the #2 filbert, vertically pull up broom hairs with Raw Sienna + Chocolate (1:1). The broom handle is Chocolate. When the broom hair is dry, add a few hairs of Raw Sienna. Highlight the broom handle with Raw Sienna + Chocolate (1:1) + a touch of Ultra White added.

Finishing
Mix Satin Glaze about the size of a quarter with a couple drops of Thinner. With the 3/8" Wee Mop, apply a coat of this over the ornament.

Apply 14K Gold to the outside edge of the ornament.

31

Porcelain Ornament: Wishing Upon a Star

Palette
Delta Air-Dry PermEnamel
14K Gold
Burnt Sienna
Chocolate
Harvest Orange
Hunter Green
Light Peach
Marshmallow
Midnight
Raw Sienna
Red Iron Oxide
Silver Smoke
Ultra Black
Ultra White
Air-Dry PermEnamel Retarder
Air-Dry PermEnamel Satin Glaze
Air-Dry PermEnamel Surface Conditioner
Air-Dry PermEnamel Thinner

Brushes
Silver Brush Limited
Golden Natural Series 2002S #2 Bright
Golden Natural Series 2003S #2 Filbert
Golden Natural Series 2006S 1/8", 1/4" Angular
Golden Natural Series 2008S 3/4" Square Wash
Ultra Mini Series 2407S #20/0 Script
Silver Wee Mop Series 5319S 1/8", 3/8"
Crystal Series 6807S #10/0 Script Liner

Supplies
Porcelain star (#ST-1), available from Gold Seal Products or wood star, item #207-0274 available from Viking Woodcrafts, Inc. (See PermEnamel Color Conversion Chart in General Instructions for painting on wood with Ceramcoat paints.)
Bubble palette used with palette paper
Grey transfer paper

Preparation
See General Instructions. Use the 3/4" Square Wash brush to apply the Surface Conditioner. Transfer design with grey transfer paper.

Instructions
Sky
To basecoat the sky area, use the 1/4" angular brush along with the 1/8" Wee Mop brush. Dress the 1/4" angular brush with Retarder and blot lightly on a paper towel. Float Midnight around the boy and dog, doing a small section at a time, and tap the outside edges of the float with the Wee Mop to soften. Continue to base the rest of the ornament with pitty-pat strokes, and tap as you go. This will give you a faux-finish effect. Let dry. Repeat this step three times, being sure it dries between each application. On the third time, add a little Ultra White with the Midnight to the highlight area on the top right.

Dog and Boy
The dog is based with two coats of Raw Sienna. With the #2 filbert, basecoat the boy's hat and pants with Silver Smoke. His jacket is based with Red Iron Oxide. Using the #2 filbert, basecoat his face Light Peach with a touch of Burnt Sienna added, to make a Dark Flesh color. With the #2 Bright brush, basecoat his scarf Midnight + Hunter Green + a touch of Ultra White (1:1: t).

Using the 1/8" angular brush, shade his face under his hairline by adding a touch more Burnt Sienna to the face base mix. Let dry. Add a touch of blush to his cheek by adding a touch of Red Iron Oxide to the shade mix.

Hat & Pants
Using the #20/0 Ultra Mini Script brush, apply very short hairs to the hat. With the 1/8" angular brush, shade the hat with Silver Smoke + a touch of Ultra Black. Highlight the hat with Silver Smoke + Ultra White (1:1). The second shade is a very soft tint of Chocolate. The pompom on his hat is Red Iron Oxide + Chocolate (1:1). Using the #20/0 Ultra Mini Script, apply short strokes of Red Iron Oxide + Harvest Orange, then some Harvest Orange + Ultra White. Using the 1/8" angular brush, shade the pants the same way as the hat.

Jacket
Using the 1/4" angular brush, shade his jacket with Red Iron Oxide + Chocolate (1:1). The first highlight is Red Iron Oxide + Harvest Orange. Apply a second highlight of Harvest Orange, but do not extend it out as far as the first. Re-enforce the shade in the V areas with Chocolate.

Hair
Stroke in his hair with the #20/0 script liner and Raw Sienna + Chocolate (1:1). Shade the hair underneath his hat with Chocolate. Pull a few highlights with Raw Sienna + a touch of Ultra White added.

Shoes
Using the #2 Bright, basecoat his shoes with Ultra Black and highlight them with Ultra Black + a touch of Ultra White added.

Dog, continued
With the 1/8" angular brush, shade the dog with Raw Sienna + Chocolate (1:1). His eyes and nose are Ultra Black. Highlight his nose with a touch of Silver Smoke.

Snow
The snow is built-up applications of Marshmallow + a touch of Midnight, then just Marshmallow. At the very tops of the snow mounds, add a little Ultra White.

Stars
The stars are first basecoated using the #10/0 liner and Ultra White. Let dry. Go over them with Raw Sienna. Add Ultra White dots in the centers. On the large star, before applying the Raw Sienna, float a haze of Ultra White around the center of the star.

Pine Boughs

Using the #20/0 Ultra Mini Script, apply the pine boughs with strokes of Hunter Green + Ultra White. Add more Ultra White to the needles at the ends of the boughs that are near the boy. Add a touch of Raw Sienna + Chocolate (1:1) to some of the branches.

Snow, continued

Tap some snow on his shoes and pants with the #2 filbert, and tap a little on the dog.

Finishing

Mix Satin Glaze about the size of a quarter with a couple drops of Thinner. Apply a coat of this over the ornament with the 3/8" Wee Mop.

Apply 14K Gold to the outside edge of the ornament.

33

Porcelain Ornaments: Patriotic

Palette
Delta Air-Dry PermEnamel
14K Gold
Chocolate
Light Burgundy
Maize
Marshmallow
Midnight
Raw Sienna
Red Red
Air-Dry PermEnamel Retarder
Air-Dry PermEnamel Satin Glaze
Air-Dry PermEnamel Surface Conditioner
Air-Dry PermEnamel Thinner

Brushes
Silver Brush Limited
Golden Natural Series 2000S #5/0, #2 Round
Golden Natural Series 2003S #2 Filbert
Golden Natural Series 2006S 1/8", 1/4" Angular
Golden Natural Series 2008S 3/4" Square Wash
Ultra Mini Series 2430S #5/0 Tear Drop
Silver Wee Mop Series 5319S 1/8", 3/8"

Supplies
Porcelain star (#ST-1) and miniature ornaments, available from Gold Seal Products or wood star, item #207-0274 available from Viking Woodcrafts, Inc. (See PermEnamel Color Conversion Chart in General Instructions for painting on wood with Ceramcoat paints.)
Bubble palette used with palette paper
Red, white, and blue transfer paper
Wedge cosmetic sponge

Preparation
See General Instructions.
Wash ornament with soap and water, rinse well, and dry. Apply Surface Conditioner with the 3/4" wash brush and let dry.

Instructions
Stripes and Blue Area
Transfer only the curved center line and stripes with Red transfer paper. The floating medium used for the ornaments is the Retarder. Using the 1/4" angular brush, float the inside edge of each of the red stripes. By using the 1/4" angular brush, you should have the entire stripe covered when you are through, with the inside a little lighter. Let dry. Before shading the stripes, it is best to base the blue area, to give this time to thoroughly dry.

Float across the top of the red stripe. Repeat this step at least three times to give a good coverage, being sure it dries well between coats. The white stripes are the porcelain itself.

Base the blue area by pitty-patting with Midnight plus a touch of Retarder. Work on a small section at a time and use the 1/8" Wee Mop to pounce lightly to soften, working first on the outside edges where you have stopped. Let dry. Repeat two to three times for good coverage. This gives it a textured look.

Shade the red stripes with floats of Light Burgundy. With the 3/8" Wee Mop, float Midnight lightly across the stripes, underneath the blue area, and if needed, use the Mop brush to soften and fade out any harsh edges of the float. Let dry.

Transfer the rest of the pattern with white transfer paper.

Holly, Leaves, and Stars
Basecoat the holly and leaves with Marshmallow. Using the #5/0 Ultra Mini Tear Drop brush, base the stars Marshmallow.

Re-base the holly and leaves with Raw Sienna + a touch of Maize. Shade the holly and leaves with Raw Sienna + Chocolate (1:1). Highlight them with Maize. Apply a second shade in the V areas with Chocolate. Go over the highlighted areas with 14K Gold. Shade the Marshmallow berries with 14K Gold. Let dry.

At this time apply a coat of Satin Glaze with a drop of Thinner added, over the entire ornament. Let dry. This helps the transfer paper to adhere better when transferring the lettering.

Lettering
Transfer the lettering with blue transfer paper. Using the #5/0 round, base the lettering with Midnight + a touch of Ultra Black added.

Miniatures
The little ornaments are based with Raw Sienna + Chocolate + 14K Gold (1:1:1), plus a touch of Retarder. Use the #2 filbert. After you have them based, let them set for a few seconds, and then wipe them lightly with the cosmetic sponge.

Finishing
Mix Satin Glaze about the size of a quarter with a couple drops of Thinner. Apply a coat of this over the ornament with the 3/8" Wee Mop brush.

God Bless America

God Bless Our Troops

35

Miss Liberty

Palette
Delta Air-Dry PermEnamel
Burnt Sienna
Chocolate
Dark Goldenrod
Ivory
Light Peach
Midnight
Raw Sienna
Red Red
Silver Smoke
Ultra Black
Ultra White
Air-Dry PermEnamel Retarder
Air-Dry PermEnamel Satin Glaze
Air-Dry PermEnamel Surface Conditioner
Air-Dry PermEnamel Thinner

Brushes
Silver Brush Limited
Golden Natural Series 2000S #5/0 Round
Golden Natural Series 2003S #6 Filbert
Golden Natural Series 2006S 1/8", 1/4", 1/2" Angular
Golden Natural Series 2008S 3/4" Square Wash
Ultra Mini Series 2407S #20/0 Script
Ultra Mini Series 2430S #5/0 Tear Drop
Crystal Series 6807S #10/0 Script Liner

Supplies
Porcelain Bisque Plate, Item #HO37PB, available from Brenda Stewart
Bubble palette used with palette paper
Small cosmetic sponge
White and grey transfer paper

Instructions
Wash and dry the surface. Apply Surface Conditioner with the 3/4" wash brush. Let dry. Apply a coat of Satin Glaze mixed with a couple of drops of Thinner to the plate. Let dry. This will act as the basecoat.

Face, Neck, and Arms
Lightly transfer the pattern with grey transfer paper, omitting the facial features and the stars on the flag at this time.

As you are painting, always have a touch of Retarder on the brush along with the paint. This will keep the painting looking soft and help you to float color and basecoat easier.

With the #6 filbert brush, lightly basecoat the flesh areas with Light Peach + a touch of Ivory added. Let dry. Transfer the facial features lightly.

Using the #10/0 liner brush, go over the tracing lines of her facial features, arms, and fingers with Light Peach + a touch of Burnt Sienna (makes a Dark Flesh color).

Using the 1/4" angular brush, shade her face, arms, and neck with the Dark Flesh Mix. Highlight her face, neck, and arms with Light Peach + a touch of Ultra White added. The blush areas are the Dark Flesh Mix + a touch of Red Red. The blush is applied over the shade areas here and there.

With the #5/0 round, base her eyes with Burnt Sienna. The whites of her eyes are Ultra White with just a touch of Ivory added to dull the Ultra White a bit. Outline the pupil with Raw Sienna + Chocolate (1:1). This same mix is used, weakened a bit with Thinner, to apply the little lashes on the bottom and strengthen the color on the eyebrows a bit. This color is also applied to her nostrils (just a tad). Shade the top of her pupil with the 1/8" angular brush and Ultra Black. Highlight the bottom of her pupil with the following Beige Mix: Dark Goldenrod + Ivory + Chocolate (2:2:1).

This Beige Mix is the color of her clothing and also is used to shade around her and the outside of the plate. Fill one full bubble in the palette with this mix, so you will have enough when the time comes to use it. Don't forget to add a drop or two of Retarder to it, so it will not dry out. The highlight shine in her eye is Ultra White. With the #10/0 liner brush, outline her upper eyelid with Chocolate and add a few lashes. Her lips are based in the Dark Flesh color. Let dry. Add a tint of the blush color to her upper lip. When this is dry, go back and darken the corners of her mouth with the same color. Her teeth are Ultra White with just a tiny bit of Ivory added.

Her Clothing
Using the 1/4" angular brush, base-tint all of her beige areas with the Beige Mix. Work the color into the areas a bit, leaving the background color of the plate as the highlight. As you get near an area that you want to fade out, lightly press with the cosmetic sponge. Strengthen the V areas a bit with a light tint of Raw Sienna + Chocolate (1:1).

The blue area is base-tinted in Midnight, gone over a few times, leaving the middle area slightly lighter for a faded look. The buttons are Red Red with beige threads in their centers.

The ribbons are based in Midnight. Shade with Midnight with just a touch of Ultra Black added. Highlight them with Silver Smoke. Add a second highlight with Ultra White.

Outline the trim area of her hat with Silver Smoke. Add the ruffle by using the 1/8" angular brush and Ultra White. Make short, little strokes, keeping the toe of the brush to the outside, toward her face. With the #20/0 Ultra Mini Script, squiggle the outline of the lace's edge in Ultra White.

Hair
With the #10/0 liner brush and thinned Raw Sienna + Chocolate (1:1), stroke in the hair in the direction of the curls. Pull some wispy hairs down from her forehead and around the side of her face on the left side. Let dry. Go over the hair again with a thin coat of the same mix, leaving some of the background showing for a highlight. Shade under the hat, under the curl, and by her neck on the left side; shade lightly near her face on the right side, all with Chocolate.

Tinting Around the Design
With the 1/2" angular brush, tint around her and the bottom portion of the flag with the Beige Mix + Retarder. Tint the sides of the plate, leaving the raised hearts and the outer edge of the scrollwork on the plate clear.

Flag
Base the handle of the flag Raw Sienna + Chocolate (1:1). Highlight the top of the finial with the Beige Mix. Shade underneath the finial and near her fingers with Chocolate. Add a few streaks of the Beige Mix on the handle in the center area for a highlight. Base the blue area of the flag with Midnight. This will take a couple of coats for good coverage. The red stripes are Red Red, and the background color of the plate is the white stripes. After the blue area is dry, transfer the stars with white graphite paper. Apply the stars with the #20/0 Ultra Mini Script and Ultra White. Shade the flag with Midnight. Add extra shading on the blue area of the flag with Midnight + a touch of Ultra Black.

Stars on the Hearts
Using the #5/0 Ultra Mini Tear Drop, paint three stars on each of the hearts, with the Beige Mix. On three of the hearts, go over one star with a thin coat of Red Red, the other with Midnight + Silver Smoke (1:1).

Finishing
Apply two coats of Satin Glaze, with a drop or two of Thinner added, over the entire plate. Let dry well between coats.

Miss Liberty

Step #1

Step #2

Step #3

38

Dots are shade areas.

39

Serenity

*This painting was inspired by the song
"As The Deer" by Martin Nystrom, "As the deer panteth for the water, so my soul longeth after Thee."*

Palette
Delta Air-Dry PermEnamel
Burnt Sienna
Chocolate
Dark Goldenrod
Hunter Green
Marshmallow
Midnight
Raw Sienna
Ultra Black
Air-Dry PermEnamel Retarder
Air-Dry PermEnamel Satin Glaze
Air-Dry PermEnamel Surface Conditioner
Air-Dry PermEnamel Thinner

Brushes
Silver Brush Limited
Golden Natural Series 2000S #2 Round
Golden Natural Series 2003S #2, #4, #8 Filbert
Golden Natural Series 2006S 1/8", 1/4" Angular
Golden Natural Series 2008S 3/4" Square Wash
Ultra Mini Series 2407S #20/0 Script Liner
Ruby Satin Series 2528S 1/8" Filbert Grass Comb
Crystal Series 6807S #10/0 Script Liner

Supplies
Plate 17" Round Scoop, Metalware Item #129-0011, available from Viking Woodcrafts, Inc.
White and grey transfer paper
Regular palette paper
2 bubble palettes
Resealable plastic bags big enough for the bubble palettes to slip into.

Instructions

Apply a coat of Surface Conditioner to the front and side of the bowl. When the painting is completed and you are ready to basecoat the back, apply Surface Conditioner before applying paint.

Mixes

Basecoat Mix, Mix #1: Midnight + Marshmallow (1:1)
Mix #2: Midnight + Hunter Green + Marshmallow (1:1:1)
Mix #3: Midnight + Hunter Green + Marshmallow (1:1:t)
Mix #4: Ultra Black + Marshmallow (1:t)
Mix #5: Ultra Black + Chocolate + Dark Goldenrod (1:1:1)
Mix #6: Dark Goldenrod + Chocolate + Marshmallow (2:1:t)
Mix #7: Mix #1 + Mix #5 (1:1)
Mix #8: Midnight + Marshmallow (2:1)
Mix #9: Midnight + Hunter Green (1:1)

Base the front and sides of the bowl with the 3/4" wash brush with the following: Mix about three half-dollar size puddles of Mix #1 with a quarter-size puddle of Satin Glaze along with a couple of drops of Retarder. The glaze helps for a smoother application of paint without streaks, and the Retarder helps prevent the mix from drying out too soon. You will use this mix also in the painting of the design.

Transfer the pattern with white transfer paper, omitting the birch trees, the deer, and the grasses. They will be transferred later.

Prepare the mixes in the bubble palettes, and add two drops of Retarder into each mix. Mix well. Also have one bubble for each of the following: Marshmallow, glazing medium with two drops of Retarder added, and Thinner only. The Thinner is used to clean the brushes between colors if needed. The sky, ground, and water are all brush-blended. As you pick up the paint, add a touch of the glazing mix to it by blending the two on the palette paper first, before applying to the surface. This will make brush-blending easier.

Sky

The sky colors are the base Mix #1, adding Marshmallow to lighten and adding Mix #2 to darken. Using the #8 filbert brush, begin horizontal strokes at the horizon line and gradually add Marshmallow to lighten as you move upward. Add more Marshmallow over the pine trees on center right. Pick up some of Mix #2 and darken on the left side of the horizon line.

Ground Area

Using the #8 filbert, begin at the horizon line. Base in the snow with Marshmallow, following the contours of the ground. As you apply Marshmallow, pick up some of the base, Mix #1, and create soft shades in the snow. The brightest areas of snow are repeated soft strokes of Marshmallow. These are gradual light applications of color to achieve depth. Allow each application to dry before adding another. With the #2 filbert, add a few footprints with little strokes of Mix #4 plus a touch of Marshmallow added. After these are dry, go over them with a thin coat of Marshmallow to mute them a bit. The rocks are based with Mix #4. Add tints of Mix #5 + #6 in the shade areas. Apply snow with short, pitty-pat strokes of Marshmallow.

Water

Using the #8 filbert brush, apply horizontal strokes of color, varying them as you work from the back to the front. Begin with Mix #2. Lighten with Marshmallow, and darken with Mix #3. Also, add some strokes of the basecoat, Mix #1. Repeated thin applications will give you a soft transition of color. Details will be applied after the rest of the pattern is transferred. Let dry.

Transfer the rest of the pattern with grey transfer paper. Omit the facial features of the deer till after you have given them the first basecoat, at which time you will transfer details with white transfer paper.

For the rest of the design, use just the Retarder as the painting medium. Dress the brush with Retarder and blot lightly on a paper towel before picking up the paint, and blend on the palette paper.

Pine Trees

Using the 1/8" angular brush, tap in the pine trees with the following colors: The farthest trees in the background are based with Mix #1 + a touch of Midnight.

The middle trees are based with Mix #1 + a touch of Hunter Green. The larger trees (two on the right and one on the left), are Mix #3. All the trees are tapped with Marshmallow after the base is tapped in, highlighted even more with Marshmallow on the side that faces the deer.

Birch Trees

Using the #4 filbert, basecoat the birch trees with Mix #4 + a touch of Marshmallow. Let dry. The smaller limbs are done with the #2 round and the #10/0 liner. (See worksheet.) With the 1/8" angular brush, sideload with Marshmallow, and stroke horizontally across the tree, beginning at the highlighted side of the tree. (See worksheet.) Add marks of Mix #4 here and there, using the #2 round. Using the 1/4" angular, apply tints of Mix #6. With the 1/8" angular brush, apply snow on the branches and sides of the trees with Marshmallow. The trees in the front are lighter than those in the back.

Deer

Using the #2 filbert, base the deer with the following mixes, in the direction of their hair growth.
Buck: Mix #5
Antlers: Mix #6 + a touch of Marshmallow
Doe and Fawn: Mix #5 + Dark Goldenrod (1:1)
Let dry, then transfer the facial features with white transfer paper.

Buck

Using the #2 filbert and not much paint on the brush, re-base the deer with Mix #6, pat-blending in the direction of hair growth. Shade by pat-blending in more of Mix #5, and strengthen shading with a touch of Mix #4. Base his eyes and nose with Mix #4. Add a sparkle in his eyes with Marshmallow. Sideload the 1/8" angular brush, then apply Marshmallow around his eyes and nose and a thin application in his ears, leaving an outside edge of the ears showing. Shade the inside of his ears with Mix #5. Using the #20/0 Ultra Mini Script, pull up some Marshmallow hairs on the edges of his ears, and stroke hairs under his chin. Let dry, then pat-blend over the hairs with the 1/8" angular brush and Marshmallow, keeping the toe of the brush under his chin. This is just to fill in the hair a bit. There is also Marshmallow on his belly, applied with the #2 filbert. His antlers are shaded with Mix #4 and highlighted with Marshmallow. There are other tints on the buck, but we will apply them after the other two deer are done.

Doe

The doe is done the same way as the buck. The only difference is the first basecoat, which gives the deer a slight difference in color.

Fawn
The fawn is done the same also, except with a little pat-blending of Mix #5 on his back. Apply thin Marshmallow spots on his back. If they appear too stark, go over them lightly with Mix #6. Highlight the fawn's back with thinned Marshmallow.

Strengthen the shading on all three deer with Mix #5 again in the V areas. This is done lightly. It will not take much. There are tints of Raw Sienna on the lightest areas of the deer and tints of Burnt Sienna on the shaded areas of their legs, the doe's and fawn's rump, the buck's belly on the left by his leg, and a touch on the very tops of their heads. These tints are to warm the color up a bit.

Water, continued
The ripples in the water around the fawn drinking are done with the #2 filbert and Mix #1. To make it appear as if there is ice around the edge of the water, use the #8 filbert to pull out thin wisps of Marshmallow. Dress the 1/4" angular brush with Retarder, and blot lightly. Tint the edges (right on top of the ice) near the ground with Midnight + Hunter Green + a touch of Ultra Black. Go along the water's edge near the ground, pitty-patting and extending out a bit here and there. Pick up some of Mix #6 and pitty-pat in. Tints of Burnt Sienna are tapped in here and there.

Grasses
Using the 1/8" Filbert Grass Comb brush first, pull up grasses with Mixes #6 and #7, then add some with the #10/0 liner brush. Add a touch of Mix #5 near the base of the grasses on the larger clumps. Tap in more snow at their base.

Shadow on Water Under Fallen Limbs
The broken limb in the front has a shadow in the water done with Mix #4. Then go over the bottom of the stroke with Mix #2 to soften it out.

Shading Around the Picture
To achieve a soft shade around the rim of the plate, use the glazing mix as the medium along with Mix #8 and work into the picture a bit. I used a #8 filbert, along with another clean brush with just glazing mix on it, to soften the edges as I went along. After this is dry, use this same mix and paint the rim and the back of the bowl.

Finishing
Using the 3/4" wash brush, apply two coats of Satin Glaze with a couple of drops of Thinner added over the entire bowl.